Regalos

Regalos

Elisa A. Garza

ISBN: 978-1-962148-16-0
LOC: 2024949396
Editor: Christine Osborne
Author Photo: Danny Nguyen

Lamar University Literary Press
Beaumont, TX

Muchas gracias a mi familia por los cuentos, las memorias, y la confianza.

You are the ones who first told me stories.
Thank you for allowing me to tell the stories I wanted to tell in the ways I wanted to tell them.

Recent Poetry from Lamar University Literary Press

Lisa Adams, *Xuai*
Walter Bargen, *Radiation Diary: Return to the Sea*
Christine Boldt, *In Every Tatter*
Devan Burton, *A Room for Us*
Jerry Bradley, *Collapsing into Possibility*
Mark Busby, *Through Our Times*
Julie Chappell, *Mad Habits of a Life*
Stan Crawford, *Resisting Gravity*
Glover Davis, *Academy of Dreams*
Wendy Dunmeyer, *My Grandmother's Last Letter*
Chris Ellery, *Elder Tree*
Kelly Ann Ellis, *The Hungry Ghost Diner*
Dede Fox, *On Wings of Silence*
Alan Gann, *That's Entertainment*
Larry Griffin, *Cedar Plums*
Lynn Hoggard, *First Light*
Michael Jennings, *Crossings: A Record of Travel*
Markham Johnson, *Dear Dreamland*
Betsy Joseph & Chip Dameron, *Relatively Speaking*
Jim McGarrah, *A Balancing Act*
J. Pittman McGehee, *Nod of Knowing*
David Meischen, *Caliche Road Poems*
Laurence Musgrove, *A Stranger's Heart*
Benjamin Myers, *The Family Book of Martyrs*
Janice Northerns, *Some Electric Hum*
Godspower Oboido, *Wandering Feet on Pebbled Shores*
Dave Oliphant, *Summing Up: Selected Poems*
Nathanael O'Reilly, *Landmarks*
Carol Coffee Reposa, *Sailing West*
Jan Seale, *Particulars*
Steven Schroeder, *the moon, not the finger, pointing*
C.W. Smith, *The Museum of Marriage*
Vincent Spina, *The Sumptuous Hills of Gulfport*
W.K. Stratton, *Betrayal Creek*
Ken Waldman, *Sports Page*
Loretta Diane Walker, *Ode to My Mother's Voice*
Dan Williams, *At the Gates, a Refuge of Milkweed and Sunflowers*
Jonas Zdanys, *The Angled Road*

For information on these and other Lamar University Literary
Press books go to www.Lamar.edu/literarypress

Acknowledgments

I wish to thank the editors of the following journals, chapbooks, and anthologies for publishing these poems, some of them in slightly different versions:

Amarillo Bay
Between the Light/entre la claridad
Bilingual Review/Revista Bilingüe
Blue Mesa Review
Boundless, Rio Grande Valley International Poetry Festival
Chachalaca Poetry Review
Concho River Review
Diagram
Earth's Daughters
Familia
Flint Hills Review
Friendswood Library Ekphrastic Poetry Anthology
Houston International Poetry Anthology
Houston Poetry Fest Anthology
Improbable Worlds, Texas and Louisiana Poets
Mom Egg Review
New Texas
PRISM International
Southwestern American Literature
Untamable City, Poems on the Nature of Houston
U.S. Latino Living Archives
Voces

For specific help with many of these poems, as well as the early versions of this manuscript, I thank Bruce Weigl and Robin Becker. Thanks also to Erika Solberg and Karen Braucher (RIP), who commented on other versions. Maria Miranda Maloney encouraged me to keep circulating this manuscript and suggested it might find a home at Lamar University Literary Press.

For financial assistance while writing these poems, I thank The Pennsylvania State University, The Texas Commission on the Arts, The Mary Anderson Center for the Arts, and The Alfredo Cisneros Del Moral Foundation.

Contents

I

I forge myself

This Is How You Cook Rice
Corpus Christi, 1989

for my mother

You watch and do.
When you are tall enough,
about nine years old, you stir and stir
to keep the grains from burning.
Your mamá has already tossed
long grained arroz into a sartén
with the right amount of oil,
which you will learn to gauge.
At twelve, you stir and watch,
let her know when the grains are castaño,
toasted brown, like apple seeds.
She will add cebolla and green bell pepper
she chopped into rectangles the size
of her fingernails. You can add the water.
You know how much, as you know
how much arroz and oil, but you let her watch.
In a few years she still watches you chop,
because she thinks you are not ready.
By twenty-one, you have watched enough.
While Abuela supervises, you cook rice
for twenty. She makes you
chop cebolla and pepper smaller,
her arthritic hands too old for the knife.
You stir to avoid further browning,
while she smashes ajo in the molcajete
con comino seeds. Un poquito de agua,
to loosen the mash from the molcajete,
and you pour it in as sharp smelling steam
billows up like church incense.
Then the tomate, not too much,
y la agua, sal, y pimienta before the lid.
Afterwards, pleased with your fluffy grains
tinted pale naranja, not sticky or burned,
Abuela says, *Now you can get married.*

Soy chicana, or Feminism for the Twenty First Century

Soy chicana,
a feminine powerful
romantic with baby-ready
arms and kickboxer legs.

Soy chicana,
and I forge myself
woman—mujer.
I am: hija—poet—
hermana—teacher—
activist—aunt—
madre—
feminista—
esposa.

Soy chicana,
a philosopher,
I step high and strong,
pressing my path
into the soft ground, free
of the sharp stones and cactus needles
that stuck my mothers and sisters.

Grandfather's Hands
Katy, 1992

My father in maroon cap and gown
sits on the trunk of a fifty-nine Chevy,
his face under the flat graduation cap
like my youngest brother's with his thick eyebrows,
long pointy chin. In my father's lap,
thumbs curve outward like shoehorns,
Grandfather's hands, thick fingers
that knew the prick of cotton pods,
a mule's weight on the reins,
the thud thud of a hoe.
If hands are the place of knowing,
my thin fingers are Abuela's,
hands that knead masa into tortillas
crisping on the stove.
My hands also tell this story:
How Grandfather's hands dropped his mug
with a thud on the table after each drink,
a call for attention, el hombre
commanding his woman's hands to bring him café,
and más tortillas. My own thuds on the table
bring my father, sleepy and confused,
looking for his papá, hand holding the mug,
or a tortilla stuffed with chorizo.

Answering Los machos

¡Ay, que linda!
What have you noticed, feo?
Soy más que mi cuerpo.

Oye chica, eres lo que comes—
vámonos a comer.
Oye, muchacho, do I look hungry?

¡Mamí! Looking good!
¿Sí, y que pendejo?
Soy una mujer bella e inteligente.

¿Ay, chaparrita, quieres bailar? Soy el mejor,
better than you've ever had.
¿De veras? ¿De veras?

Oye, muchacha, tengo lo que quieres—
anything you want.
¿Y qué tienes guapo?

Quiero un hombre confiado,
someone who will talk to me
cara a cara, serio, que me ponga atención.

¿Mira chica, adónde vas?
Yo sé adónde voy,
and what I'll do when I get there.

¿Y tú?

All Señoritas Get Married
Corpus Christi, 1965

    for my mother

She carries this knowledge
deep, in her gut,
the way she will one day
carry her babies, hidden and small,
the phrases sometimes tingling her ears
as she changes sheets
and empties bedpans at the hospital,
sometimes roaring after the doctors
thank her for translating their diagnoses
and dismiss her with a nod.

She hears the words in her head
louder than the rude man's comments on the bus,
louder even than her father saying *NO*
about going to the homecoming dance
or attending mass at the cathedral downtown.

And when her nursing school friend
is talking about her husband's brother,
the one who lives in Dallas,
she hears the words in her head louder,
and louder like a song building to the chorus:
        Las señoritas se casan.
        Todas las señoritas se casan.
        Todas las señoritas.
        Sí, también yo.

Test Drive

Do not do
that machismo thing,
that puffed-up-hombre
I'm cool thing—
you cannot ignore
this electricity
that moves arm to arm
when we touch, palm to palm.
Like two halves of a battery,
our contact is a go, a chemical start,
and papí, this engine runs,
a steady murmur of want.
A humming that lulls,
that guns for the open road.

Mucho cuidado

Father is leaving for work. Mother is home
because of the new baby. I watch him
on the couch while she irons shirt after shirt.
Hanger in her mouth like a giant fishhook,
she buttons them up, one by one. Father kisses her
on the cheek after looking at the baby
and mother says, mucho cuidado.

This was my daily lesson on affection,
back when my parents still loved each other.
Today, a man I barely know said this to me,
mucho cuidado, and affection pricked my heart,
his good-bye probing sharp and hot.

From the car, I wave at Grandma and Grandpa.
Plump as snowmen, they raise their arms
as we back out of the driveway.
Mucho cuidado, Grandma says, take care,
come back to me. Grandma to Máma to me—
our hearts learned to love this way,
to distance what we feel from what we say.

The First of Many
Corpus Christi, 1966

After they are engaged, he writes
over and over, carta tras carta,
that he will transfer his job as postal clerk
to Corpus Christi. That he would like
to live near his brother, and her family,
to see them every week, or even every day.
This promise makes her smile,
especially when her mother is sighing
while she scrubs the pots,
saying that Dallas is so far away,
muy lejos for a daughter to go.

But soon, he writes of other things,
how happy his mother is about the marriage,
how much he would like them to meet,
how glad he is to hear about the wedding dress
she bought on sale at the JC Penney.

And her mother? She will wear her sadness
about Dallas while she stirs carne guisada,
while she sweeps from front porch to back,
while she folds seven sets of clean clothes.
Even at the wedding, she carries this sadness,
her face showing it in every photograph.

Atardecer

La cara tuya, un ovalo,
a bird's nest

renewing its roundness.
Under sheets of clouds,

breeze chases my hair.
La voz tuya, the mourning dove's

melting row of low notes:
cu cu ru in my ear.

La sonrisa tuya revoloteando,
flitting light under trees,

that desire you tether inside.

My Parents at Tía Mary's House
Corpus Christi, 1967

She wears a red crepe dress
and cat's eye horn-rim glasses,

he a dark suit, white shirt,
very skinny tie.

That day, someone took a photograph
of two young people in love.

Backs to the window, they sit close, his arm
over her shoulder, her hand

holding his. In her lap, the engagement ring,
a small thing really,

hard to see. The children are still cells
hidden deep between hips.

Only smiles to see now; just two people
who will marry,

who will one day become unhappy
and stay that way.

Not a small thing, such sadness,
but it was hard to see.

Threshold

Above autumn, the moon sags,
pale stone in the sky.
You stare out the window,

eyes unfocused puddles, muddy green.
You say you fear we'll change.
Your neck and shoulders hunch. You stiffen,

as if you expect the air to sharpen,
the moon to drop from weight,
the season to suddenly shift.

Respect
Corpus Christi, 1966

Not the way things are done.
Not proper. She knows. She knows this
the way her knees know when to kneel
during mass, the way her mouth knows
to say *yes, doctor,* when she receives orders
during her shift at the hospital.
She knows he should not drive down
from Dallas and pick her up, continue driving
south into the desert to his parents' home.
She knows that he should bring them
to her, that they should sit on the brown couch,
his mother with her purse in her lap,
his father holding his hat in his hands.
She knows this drive is his own idea
because she knows his mother would not invite her
to visit over Easter this way. She knows
she must decline. Even he knows she will.
Not proper. No, not the way things are done.

To Begin Again
Kingsville, 1999

When he heard his ex's voice
mumbling on the machine,
he walked back out the door
and invited the neighbor for ice cream:
old comfort, new face.

It's a good night for sky watching, she said.
He could feel the stress going soft.
He drove her out to the marsh,
walked a graveled path to a pier,
flashlight spotting the way.
And for one moment, his hands
over hers on the binoculars,
he thought the crickets said maybe, maybe.
While she focused on Jupiter,
he squinted at the Perseid arm,
seeking in the glow,
in the comfort of milk,
the way of his heart.

Early Flight

Today the just-morning sky thickens in blues,
deep black where it smears against stars,
and clean as the Caribbean where it laps airport runways,
frosting them with fine flakes of snow.
Last night, when you asked, I told you a story,
my voice a calm ripple on the night's lake:
how the animals, shivering and afraid,
asked the Great Spirit to take away the darkness,
so he showed them the Home Star,
and taught them to make sky pictures
using sharp edged stones from the river.
Just before morning, they slipped out of the sky,
leaving their soft imprints behind
for the nights to come.
Today, I startled myself awake,
and now aboard a silver long necked goose,
I leap into this morning sky,
angling upward into the day,
away from a night where we, too,
could have searched the stream bed for stones
and tossed up a few stars to light our way.

II

throw the heart

Catherine, Making the Most of Henry V

In 1415, Henry V of England, convinced he had claim to France by inheritance, invaded. Nearly five years later, he had defeated the French armies and took the princess Catherine as his bride to seal the treaty that recognized him as heir of France.

An Invasion, An Offer

At least he is young, she thinks.
She would ask the messenger for his words,
and to tell her his looks, the way he frowned,
no laughed, at her father's meager offer.
A few minor dukedoms! She already knows
that he must have all or nothing.

The War, The Wait

Would he move over her, she wonders,
as he now rides over France, slow, and sure
only of a victorious outcome?
*Que magnifique! Surely he would make
strong love after so much war?*
She is learning the English,
to loosen her tongue from its heavy sounds,
and blushes at the looseness to come.

Consummation

She feels his hands hot in hers,
listens to his fractured French—
he is nervous, bubbling like champagne!
And she can only stare,
think of the world they will make together,
the waiting finally over.

Mangos

I sat in your lap,
our mouths puckered, each taste
a mango wince. Such tart kisses
left us wanting more.

Yet, slice after slice,
we could not find
sweetness in that fruit.
Nor I, in you.

Even so, tonight's mango
is the size and shape
of my breasts, soft heavy ovals
that recall your touch,
the suck of your fleshy mouth.

I cut soft sour moons,
throw out the yellow heart.

The Moment

"... through one man sin entered the world ..."
—Romans 5:12

If Eve was framed,
as the bumper sticker says,
only the devil could have done it,
disguised himself as her
while Eve busied herself gathering grapes.
Her perfect hand offering the apple,
fingers hugging the globed fruit
like slim leaves, she (the devil)
must have reminded Adam
of earlier gifts, posing, pupils dilated,
offering a snack that promised more
than knowledge, her words slow and sure
between ragged breaths:
Just eat the apple, Adam.
Consequently,
he must have held her hand,
the fruit to his mouth,
taken several very quick bites
with his eyes closed.

Desire

Cool sheets, I yearn for warmth,
for a body at my back.
All morning, I dream a man
with an angled face will walk
across this room, his stare
intense as the first long rain
of fall, his gaze prickly
as mosquitoes that follow.
Listen to the train howl
my solitude moonward.

I dream his eyes are sky.
I am a ragdoll, his
gaze my only clothing.
Your knock brings a circle
of arms, an open mouth.
I take what I can get.

Philomela Reads Her Weave

"[s]he set up her threads on a barbarian loom and wove
a scarlet design on a white ground, which pictured the
wrong she had suffered."
—*Ovid*, Metamorphoses, Book VI

Procne, dear sister, into this cloth
I have woven our sad story,
but the white wool will dry your tears,
as it has dried mine.
I trust these images to you,
worked on a crude loom
built from twigs and vines
pulled through the window.
Remember our servant, old Oryia,
how she taught even my stubborn fingers
to weave a scene with grace?
Her sharp voice comes back to me in chants:
The weave tells the woman's life.
The cloth reveals a woman's quality.
How we laughed under her stern looks!
Even her face would smile at such fine fabric,
a weave smooth and pure as sand.
You will recognize me in this work,
in the tight squares of my weave.

Do you perceive the royal ship and sails
and your husband's cloak (scarlet against the white)?
Father always wears stripes.
I have also outlined myself with red,
my tunic white with innocence.
See your husband Tereus charm
Father on bended knee?
He convinces Father to allow a visit.
Eager to see you, I hug my thanks.
Now I know that the gods
must be punishing us all.
The omen of Mother's death is true—
I have not escaped the tragedy of my birth.

These red crescents show the ocean—
our journey on a sea of blood.
The tower rises, also colored red

with the shame of Tereus's deeds.
Sister, I did not know how to display his violence. . .
I cannot even bear to think of it,
his heaviness on top of me like a storm.
Procne, I long to see your face.
On the voyage, I dreamed of our talks,
the walks we would take together,
arms around each other's waists,
our heads so close they touch.
Oh, to be girls again, our only trouble
setting the loom for our next tapestry.

This next part is not as clear,
but you must see: I screamed curses
at your husband for his actions,
and he cut out my tongue.
This I show you, and how I bled
and bled red from my mouth.
I traded my jewelry for thread,
and wove this sad message
under twelve quarter moons.
Dear sister, my story is told.
Come quickly, for I am done with weeping.

Winter Beach
Padre Island, 2000

A man and a woman walk the sand
only they and the gulls,
the sky four shades of blue,
horizon a white mist.
They stand in surf
under a rounding moon
dull as an antique coin,
sand sinking under their feet.

If this was a romance,
they would walk holding hands,
then watch green waves collapse
into smooth brown planes of glass.
He would stand behind her
and she would lean on him
while the wind touched
his face with her hair.

If they were strangers,
they would have walked
from opposite directions,
each stopping to watch
the cawing gulls swoop,
wind-jerked, over red guts,
fight over silver heads
left by a fisherman.

If they crossed their arms
into Xs tight and hard as pretzels,
eyes closed to the gulls, to the blues
and browns and whites of this scene,
the wind would say good-bye
for them, their mouths and ears
closed to this beach, to each other.

Neither knows how it is supposed to go.

The Marriage
1967–1998

She knew what mattered; for years she filled her role,
supported a marriage not growing so well.
He had stopped tending the fires, had darkened his soul

into an ocean of sadness, waves swollen,
cresting, pushing, pushing him until he fell.
He knew what mattered, they each filled a mold:

he made decisions, she washed every bowl.
Meantime, they moved into a marriage cell,
into darkness, isolation, where her soul

grew empty, sadder. Finally, he folded;
his words clanged in her head like broken bells.
Nothing mattered, not years of love, not their roles:

mother, lover, cook, maid, and wife, she totaled
them up on her side. His: father (sort of), pell-
mell husband, lover on the surface, soul-

mate? No. Sometimes yard man, gardener, charcoal
barbeque griller, but not partner, not well-
wisher, not what mattered. Only a role,
she realized: this was not a union of souls.

Love Poem, Years Late

for Ryan Wyatt

I.

Many nights, side by side
at your kitchen table, I loved the angle
of your chin, the color of your shadow
as you bent over textbooks and graph paper,
reviewing for comprehensive exams.
When you rose to refill our glasses,
you always filled mine to the brim,
forgetting I had only asked for *a little*.
As if, by giving me more than I'd asked,
we would somehow come out even—
balance your affection for men
with my affection for you.
Now, like the sun of a new solar system,
you surround yourself
with expanding circles of men.

II.

You never finished your study of Jupiter's ring.
I know we can never go back
to the time I wore my clothes
like heavy manuscripts
while you observed the night sky,
computed the gravity that pulled
Jupiter's ring towards, then from Io,
like waves at the beach.
An unlikely attraction you said.

III.

At the telescope on the roof of the planetarium
during the last lunar eclipse,
your arm arcs to demonstrate for the crowd
the path of the moon moving into umbra.
Your head is the earth casting shadow.
Your fist the moon revolving into darkness.
The children smile because now they understand
how gloom can obscure the moon,
and how it returns again to shine on them,
full face beaming, recognizing
the earth by its sameness, as do I.

Touch-Tag

for Tony Ragucci

Like two neighborhood kids
who meet for the first time
because they both hate the monkey bars,
we are feeling each other out,
meeting up, liking what we see.
Today, we walk to the video store,
drums thrumming into the evening,
vibrations spreading down darkening streets
the way our hearts shove blood
into the nights of our arms and legs.
We stop to listen, our heads and feet
beating forward in rhythm.
The leader smiles and nods at an extra drum,
and before I know it, you are pounding skin.
I listen to your slow notes chase the others,
their quicker beats circling so fast
they catch up with yours before sprinting off again.
And I am reminded of touch-tag,
where children circle the playground
as they tag each other "it,"
and how this game plays out with only two,
who eventually wear out and touch each other
"it" without running away,
hands slapping back and forth
between heaving breaths.
And I know this is what we do:
play touch-tag with our hearts,
the times between touches shorter and shorter.

Rap Song

let me tell you story
my folks at war now
fightin' and all that
gettin' a divorce

he says she always angry
wouldn't talk to him
she says he always quiet
wouldn't answer her
they can't talk it up
can't work it out
always warrin'
fightin' shoutin'
now divorcin'

this I learned from them
can't work things out
can't make it last
haven't found my man

but dad don't understand
yeah he asks me
when I'm gonna marry
question kinda scary
seein' how he the one
didn't work it out

he thinks I'm gettin' old
need to settle down
but this I know
don't want sadness
don't want problems
want to do it right

talk it out
work it out
make it last
make it tight

Counterpoints

The woman groups flowers in the glass vase
and soaks up the man's deep voice like a caress in her ear.
She sees herself lying next to him, inside his spoon-cradle,
his chin pushing on the top of her head,
the wind of his words blowing through her hair, her skull.
She wills his hands to press her stomach flat,
to cup her small breasts.
Then she laughs, throws her head back,
licks his chin, his teeth, the tip of his nose.

Watching her fondle daisies and violets, the man
desires the woman's fingers as flames at his back.
He tells her about his work, a movie he saw,
wills her to turn and walk right up to him.
He will breathe in and out on her neck,
sigh on her collarbone's pulse.
He wants to undress her slowly,
burnish her bare flesh smooth with his hands,
add a glaze with his hot mouth.

The Model

I am the anatomy lesson, a mass of shifting muscles drawn under skin.

I am the shaman's handprints spit-painted onto cave walls.

I am Venus afloat a shell boat.

Under the weight of jeweled headdress, bracelets thick at my wrists and ankles, I pose.

I am Virgin Mary, my flat elongated face holy with golden halo, my lap throning the baby body of Christ.

I am at my dressing table, reflected in the mirror, arms like wings beside my head as I pin my hair.

I am the bulbous mother figurines.

I am every aristocrat's wife, eyes staring from portrait galleries, from above the mantels.

Without me, there is nothing. I am canvas, paint, artist.

I am "Nude Descending a Staircase" in cubist vision, light refracted and refracted, so that the stairs bend around me, like a blanket.

I am Helga: always, he wanted to paint.

I am Mona Lisa; my eyes see forever.

I am Nagel's wife, pop art princess.

The ship's prow, I lead the way, wind-blown hair filled with salt.

I am the nude, the blue, the red. Picasso never saw me.

I am Eve, the apple in my hand, already cold.

I am the reflection you won't find in the mirror. Ask Frida about self-portraits.

I am the ballerinas, the dances Degas could never learn.

I am every breast on every canvas.

Desert Story

There is a body in the desert
outside Juarez, a woman's body
with hands tied too tightly, a silent story
swollen and purple, waiting on the sand.
Women's words that only the cactuses
know, a story of bodies, of women.

Where are the missing women
of Juarez? Clues hide in the desert
among nopales and maguey, cactuses
standing silent while bodies
bleed, clothes thrown on the sand.
Details lost in the winds, words that tell the story.

Violence echoes the story,
words in the minds of the women
who walk across this sand
on their way to work, the desert
silent about all the bodies,
the danger sharp as fine needles on cactus.

Who shoots holes through cactuses,
writing another chapter in the story?
Where are the storytellers, those silent bodies?
What cleans the blood the women
leave like words in the desert;
who reads their stories from the sand?

They are there still: silent sands
full of stories like cactuses
full of needles, the desert
collecting a book of stories,
each story the words of a different woman,
each woman placing her body

in the table of contents, a body
of work poured onto the sand.
Violence echoes in the minds of women,
words that prick silently as cactus
needles, more needles for lost stories
of women left bleeding in the desert,

bodies prone like Sonora cactuses,
sands drifted over them in layered stories,
women of words, lost in the desert.

Canto

Because you are sick,
I lie awake next to you,
listen to you breathe,
your slow ins and outs of air
the harmonic whine of locusts,
sound of summer heat pressing down.

I lay under the Chinese tallow,
sun pushing through the leaves,
listened with eyes closed
to the hum from above,
its rhythm pressing down.
I waited for cool wind
to lull me like a swing,
for the whisper of leaves
back and forth.

Cooler now, your breath,
like those leaves, moves
in and out, in and out.

The Landscapes That Hide You

Near-night sky,
bluest edge expanding quick as spilt ink
to meet the earth.

Morning fog
a shroud of gauze that lifts
to show your faces.

Splash, splash of waves,
relentless whispers,
the very beats of your hearts.

III

los recuerdos, the memories

Border Sonnet

When you live in South Texas, you hear como
que no as often as why not and your ears
don't notice when the tongue speaking to you
slides over, flúido, smooth as wax paper
to say: bueno, bye; see you mañana.
Or, hasta, girlfriend; call me apenas.
Our bilingual speaking, our code switching,
our back-and-forth movements: we are combining
culturas. Es la vida, simplemente.
En las fronteras, we live between, entre
lenguas, countries, economies, between
the lines, in the grey areas, más o menos.
Language has no borders, no geography.
It dances where it wishes, map or no.

Canción

Jose Antonio Contreras, 1923—1925, Campbellton

Hermana helped you, Tío Jose,
with breakfast, tore the tortilla
into spoons for blanquillos y fríjoles
that she pushed into your mouth.
Afterwards, she helped with your chinelas,
tied the black laces twice.

Outside, Tío, your brothers fed pollitos
while your tongue clucked them *tchoi tchoi* quiet.
You gathered pecans in the sharp grass
by the train tracks, filled your pockets
with the small ones, los chiquitos.

You stared at that snake, clucked *tchoi tchoi*,
laughing your baby laugh at the rattle.
And when you howled,
your brothers carried you to the house,
little pecans dropping from your pockets.
In the rocker, Mamí held you tight
as your world shrank to pain and motion,
and as your sister cried louder than you
because she hadn't pulled your socks
up to hide your calves, swollen now,
and red from the snake's taste of you.

Two Januarys

Central Pennsylvania

This far north, days lengthen just as winter eases,
cold, into my mind, and I'm delirious
at the dinner-time light, the day's brief melt,
and pink ringlets of cloud in an almost-blue sky.
On a short walk, I see the high slim limbs
of Dutch elms whose dark knobby-fingered hands claw
against the sky's soft glow.
I dare myself to record winter light, clouds, trees,
simple and straightforward.

South Texas, 1998

This far south, I could celebrate New Year's
with a barbecue—it's hot enough for cut-off shorts
and bare feet. I open doors and windows to fresh air,
sit on the balcony. As tall palms totter
in brisk winds, the dried fronds of their skirts
whisper an endless soothing song. All day,
the sun plays hide-n-seek with cream puff clouds,
their quick paths across the sky the only signs
of winter to record.

Story
Escobares, 1948

They were still shorter than their hoes,
two boys, my Tío Roberto and my father.
But they were scraping the dirt into little hills,
those long hoe handles wiggling above their heads.
It was February, y Delfina the mule,
she had pulled the plow over la tierra twice,
so the work was not so hard.
Pero, it could never go fast enough for niños
eager for the good weather, talking only of béisbol.
That year, they were in charge of making the first pelota,
and they planned to make the bestest, longest lasting one.
Hombre, no one had money for a real baseball
(in fact, no one they knew had ever seen one),
so they saved their torn up t-shirts all year,
took hilo from their mamá and some extra cuerda
that was used to tie up the bales of cotton.
During games, a homerun hit would bust that ball—
I mean, pieces of string and strips of dirty cotton
would float all over their heads.
No one ever hit a homerun without busting the ball,
although these boys of Escobares, they often argued
about hits that bounced off nopales in the outfield,
the balls flying out all full of spines.
Entonces, during one of these ball making conversations,
when perhaps Papá was insisting that alternating layers
of cotton and string would make the strongest ball,
the hoe slipped and sliced a red stripe on his ankle.
Well, Roberto knew their father would accept no excuse
if the corn wasn't planted before la luna turned around to see it.
Ojale, he could hear him already: *ustedes no sirvan para nada!*
So, he spit on the ground and stopped that bleeding with mud,
and they kept going down the rows, making hills.
Pues, by the time their papá found out,
hijo de dios, there was nothing else to do.
The ankle was a mess, the foot already swollen all ugly,
and they still had to plant the corn.
Fíjates, Abuelo had to pour his licor on that cut,
all of it, y mi papá, he spent a week making that pelota.

Sunflowers
Driscoll, 1997

Los mirasoles duck their small heads,
repeating and repeating nods of recognition.
It has been more than a year
since I last drove this road,
Route 665 through fields bordered by weeds.
More than a year since these look-at-the-sun flores
caught my eyes in their spider web of stems,
that graceful network of leaves and thin strands.
Their high necks bounce in the wind,
jerking and jerking like crazed swans.

As I watch them whizz by the window,
I know I have come home to la tierra,
these fields heavy with the white of ripe cotton,
y los recuerdos, the memories.

Song of Migrant Work

German Garza IV, 1897–1977

I.

When I was eight, Abuelo lay dying
in the bed la familia paid for by the day.
He wore the whitest clothes he'd ever owned
and my father kept telling stories,
cuentos of his childhood.
I remember the red wagon
because like my father in the story,
I could hear the wagon wheels
clatter on the gravel road
as my grandfather pulled it home.
Dad had told this story many times before:
I knew Abuelo bought the wagon
where he filled the jug, how mi papá
y mis tíos played and played with it
until the wheels fell off.

II.

My father first heard family stories
during long truck drives,
summer after summer,
when children, men, and women
packed themselves tightly for the trip to harvest,
each family huddled around the chests,
the wooden boxes of dishes and colchas.
For days, they traveled like this
as far as Arkansas or Oklahoma
stuck together with only talk
y cuentos de familia to pass time.
My father loved the stories from this life,
passed on cuentos and family voices to us
when we drove between Houston and Roma,
the car and his voice traveling the distance
between his childhood and ours.

III.

Early June, a child watched the road
from the shade of the last orange tree,
noting the movement of each dust cloud,
looking for the truck with high slatted walls
covered by lanterns, buckets, washboards,
and barrels of water. It stopped for Los Garcias,
y Los Escobares, collecting families
one by one. *Allí viene, allí viene,*
and everyone grabbed bundles.
Grandfather only knew the migrant life;
he trained his children to chase the cotton,
to pick their way back home to el valle year after year.
He needed his jug like he needed their work, to survive.

IV.

Summer Saturdays, paydays,
they put on good clothes
and used each other as mirrors
to comb their wet hair into waves.
When Papá returned, their brown faces grinned,
waiting as he counted out for frijoles, arroz,
harina, y kerosen into Mamá's smooth palms.
He asked Tío Roberto and my father:
M'ijos, how much did you pick this week?
More than last time, more than sus hermanas?
Only seven and eight years old,
slow with their small sacks sewn from old shirts,
they nodded quickly, *Sí Papá.*
With their quarters, they bought hamburgers,
fries and cokes, a funny book,
watched Roy Rogers and The Lone Ranger.
When their father returned, late Saturday nights,
singing to himself as he walked,
his money sloshed in the jug.

V.

At eleven years old, my father
raced his brothers down the rows,
learning to pick faster, to pick more,
his brown hands filling the long sack that trailed

behind him like a giant windsock.
A few years later, he was the one;
he filled the sack five times a day.
By then, sus hermanos had left
with the army, or picked for their own families.
And Grandfather watched his youngest provide,
the sacks filling stomach and jug, week after week.

VI.

The summer my father was fifteen,
he decided to quit. For years,
he had returned to el valle en Octubre,
beginning school a month late,
the only Garza to go to high school.
He told his papá that he had missed
too much, that he would stay
for the entire season, not go to school.
That night, my grandfather
threw his jug against a giant scrub oak
that cracked the old glass, liquor
seeping into the tree through its roots.

VII.

During the first visit I remember,
Abuelo slumped in the wheelchair
parked beside the rest home's fountain,
my brother and I on either side of him.
When Dad took our picture,
Grandfather never moved his arm to touch us,
never moved his head to look at us.
I remember the way his legs leaned sideways,
thin boards too long for the footholds
of the chair, the way his thick fingers
hung from his hands like limp leaves,
his white hair glinting in the sun.
I think about the stories I've been told,
how picking cotton tears the skin
off your fingers, how the sun makes you sweat
como un overworked animal. How your back aches
from bending over, from carrying the sack
to the scales. How your knees almost never
straighten from hunching down the rows.
How you look forward to Saturday,
the day you can wear yourself out with play.

VIII.
Falfurrias, 1990

Years after my grandfather's funeral,
we drove by cotton fields picked by machine,
and Dad pointed out plants still heavy,
waving his arm toward the rows.
I imagined tíos y tías stooping
with their heavy homemade sacks,
brown against the white of cotton.
The machines, they don't pick like we did;
we cleaned the field. And Dad chased
my brother into the field,
taught him to pull puffs from stems,
one small clump at a time.

IX.

This is un poquito de la familia,
a gift of cuentos they have passed on.
We know these cuentos, hear these stories,
and we share a love for cotton cloth,
my brothers, my cousins, and I.
The cotton is the easy part—
we wear it so close to our skin
that we barely notice its soft touch.
And like the alcohol that runs in our blood,
the migrant work that brought us here,
cotton tells us who we are.

Family Wedding
Austin, 1994

In the photograph on the wall,
the relatives pose, los tíos
con una tía, madre del novio,
hermanos wearing ties and dark suits,
cowboy hats and boots,
la tía dressed in green to the right.
Each aunt and uncle stands up straight,
a group of thick trees. Tía dice,
¿Que bueno, what a nice picture, no?
No one remembers that I took the drinks
from each uncle's hand, moved them carefully
to the white tablecloth.

Cabrito
Escobares, 1974

Our uncles bought a black goat,
tied it to the mesquite tree
by Grandpa's shed. We stared,
my cousin, my brother, and I,
niñitos wondering why they'd tied him up,
but the men would not answer.
Together again, the uncles laughed,
told stories in their loud Spanish,
while drinking beer.

The young goat bleated and hobbled
an arc at the end of its rope.
We ran as close as we dared,
to pet him, but the uncles
said deja lo, leave him alone.

The next day, after our egg hunt,
after busting cascarónes,
egg shells and confetti in our hair,
we crowded into the yellow kitchen
for plates of arroz, frijoles, y tacos:
dark strips of meat,
fresh chile, tomate.
So many of us gathered there
that we crowded onto the porches,
todos, un grupo grande,
eating el cabrito in sunshine.

Searching for Continuity
Richmond, 1995

> *for my father*

Monotony of cotton,
heat sweats into my torn, sore fingers.
The bag drags heavy.
Work the way work should be.
Day after day after day, place after place,
the same from Tulsa to Falfurrias.
Not this stuff at the post office—
desk, computer, phone.
Cotton no longer grows in these fields
around the post office
where I sweat among the mail.
Today, I drive to work the long way,
remembering my other truck rides,
the lull of family voices,
how even as we drove to fields
farther and farther from home
familia y comunidad estuvieron lo mismo,
todo estuvo mismo, always the same.

Some days I just want to keep driving,
más allá de este trabajo, este mundo,
all of it that changes and grows poco a poco,
like the mail that must be delivered.
I want to drive without ever stopping,
the road in front of me
moving across the windshield
of la troca mia like a big tv screen
until I arrive again con Mamá y Papá,
otra vez con la familia y los compadres,
y todo está mismo,
todo está como antes,
the same as it was:
fields of cotton before dawn,
white into the distance,
blessing the work about to begin.

The Visit
Roma, 1975

Seven-year-old summer,
back home como se dice Papá.
My cousin, brother, and I crouch over ants,
thin lines moving across driveway stones
two-way traffic over fallen peaches,
green flesh too hard and sour
for our tender tongues.
At the source of the ant river,
peaches melt into angry red lumps.

From the hallway at the home, I see Abuelo
rising up in bed to look at us,
see the hard and sour frown on his face.
He looks angry and red, like those peaches.
I hold Mamá's hand, look for ants
between the small yellow tiles of the floor.
The white lines lead to grandpa's bed,
to that rough voice asking a question
before Tía walks over and shuts the door.

Vesperal

Houston, 2000

First evening of fall since I moved
to the city, and I miss the stars.
Sickle moon winks low in the west
holding a deep wave of blue behind her.
Steady as ants, airplane lights roam north-south,
leaving no wake. I breathe deep,
the city's noises in my head, raise my arms
as if in prayer, as if to hug this sky.
I miss the friends I left behind,
the comfortable ways we knew each other,
their bright faces like the stars,
like the lights of home, like rows of sacred candles.

Quilt Squares/Cuadrados

Louisa Tanguma Reyes, 1896–1995, Campbellton

Bisabuela Louisa made jellies and tamales, quilts
and chile; for every great grandchild, she sewed a crib quilt.

Before I moved north, too far from mi familia,
my mother worked nights, hands stitching my winter quilt.

While away, I sew words, stitch los cuentos into poems,
shape los voces familiar into my own kind of quilt.

At the cemetery, six pairs of hands, nietos carried the coffin,
family gathered like a large sewing circle to make a quilt.

Como Louisa, I save unused clothes and bits of cloth,
piece and stitch them up, these bright squares my first traditional quilt.

IV

the words she writes

How to Survive a Drought
Kingsville, 1999

I picture women, narrow and bronze,
mis abuelas y tías who lived in this desert,
next to low mesquite trees with arched arms,
grinding last year's brittle corn for daily masa,
walking among cotton plants halted knee high,
and harvesting nopales that hide flesh under long spines.
While summer stretches still, life stagnates in this desert
where vacas chew cud under the same tree all day,
perros hide in water troughs till dark,
and the dust resettles on floors while you sleep.
No wonder the children grew lean and strong,
one right after the other, one for each year.
No wonder. Mis abuelas y tías, who knew
about drought, must have turned to their husbands
the last weeks of winter with deliberate passion.
Sí, they wanted to feel a child ripening towards birth,
needed their swelling stomachs as evidence among stillness
that life was moving from this long season to the next,
needed this long hope to outlast such heat.

Una mujer dice

I've never had un novio,
always dated gringos, tall pale boys
who could not speak Spanish.
Comunicación is hard enough
without stumbled palabras, my phrases
slow and heavy like rising masa, no?

¿Pero tú, hombre, quién sabe?
Are you como tus hermanos machistas?
For them, soy muy Americana,
though I don't look como las gringas.
I am one mixed-up mestizaje chicana.
I blur the lines.

Mi papá me dice que
men are hard to find.
This is his way of telling me
I am taking too long.
Posible, pero I am not looking
por un esposo; I want a partner
to cook tortillas y hacer chile,
to merengue, to talk,
cuerpo a cuerpo, mind to mind.
No quiero un machista, quiero un hombre.
¿Entiendes lo que he dicho?

Regalos

Elena Perez Garza, 1901–1992, Escobares

Sometimes, she cooked on the hearth,
a big hole in the yellow kitchen wall.
Until I was seven, she kept cows
penned behind the house.
My brother and I called her *grandma*
with the cow, abuela con vaquita.
She hung a picture of Jesucristo
against the wall where she slept.
Her cocina was yellow like masa.
She bent to wash pots and pans
under a faucet outside the kitchen door.
In the picture, Jesus wore thorns.
Loud voices woke us every morning,
and chorizo smells from her kitchen.
Grandma slept on her side,
her hands together, praying.
My brother and I slept on the floor,
behind the dividing wall.
She wrapped her head in a rag at night,
wore washed-out cotton shifts,
long dark socks, blue slippers.
After the funeral,
because I am small,
like she was,
my aunt gave me
her slips and camisoles.

Russian Woman on a Stool

My downstairs neighbor
brings her low stool
to the foot of the stairs.
A solid woman in dark gray
loosely hung over ampleness;
her head covered by a large scarf,
pale colors ring her babushka face
like a corona.
When I pass, we nod,
say nothing.
I imagine she thinks
I sleep late,
her clothes hung on the line,
the porch already swept,
borscht boiling.
I rush past her,
my hair wet, my bright dress
blowing behind me
like a flag,
my head filled with hurry.

Notes in a Blue Composition Book, July 1944

Marta Contreras Reyes, 1916–2004, Corpus Christi

The baby's squalls fill the house,
her sound fading in and out when she breaks for air,
like a warning siren. She cries because
she does not get enough leche from the breast.
My grandmother must carry her to make her stop,
must pace the rooms, arms bouncing and swaying.
Older brother Arturo, restless, follows them,
skipping and making nonsense sounds,
calling for more of their mami's attention.
My grandparents have money for once
because of the war, enough to send some home,
to the desert they left for this coastal city
named for the body of Christ,
where palm trees line all the roads like soldiers.
It is the slick sounds of the trains they miss most,
this city so loud without a background drone.
Even so, soon they will buy the white frame house
and move it to the lot on Osage street.
But first, they visit the nice white doctor
who weighs the baby, and sends them
to buy the bottles that my grandmother
will have to clean and boil and steam dry
every day before she fills them with formula.
Seeing her scrubbing and scrubbing at the sink,
Arturo jumps down the porch steps
and crosses the street, where she will find him
staring down a deep hole in the road,
as if searching for something in the darkness.
For the doctor to see at their next visit,
she writes the feedings in a blue notebook:
4 ounces, 4 ounces, only 3 ounces,
her numbers in straight columns.
She tears out a few pages to write letters
to her brothers who still fight in the war,
telling them about the new baby,
Arturo's adventure, Octavio's promotion.
She does this while the children are sleeping
under watch of the humming fan,
after she has washed the diapers and hung them
like rows of big teeth on the back porch.

As she loosens her hair from the bun,
and it flows down her back long as a promise,
she wonders if all the steamy cleaning water
is messing up her eyes when it rises to her face
because she must bend so close over the paper
to see the words she writes with the pencil.

September 2008
Houston

My Hurricane Ike story
begins at the breast,
ends at the breast.
The middle is milky too.
My newborn, two weeks old,
nurses for hours, hardly resting.
This is the storm called baby;
she thinks only of herself,
knows only the storm of hunger,
the rhythm of suckling,
a strong surge followed by calmer waves.
Because she is always at my breast,
we do not evacuate.
I am milking time, timing the milk;
time converts to milk.

My baby and I are communing,
we are nature, thinking only feed to feed.
I am too busy with now, with giving milk
to stockpile food or check our supplies.
My husband assures me we have enough.
Between nursings, I make more ice.

After night falls, I listen to the wind
while my baby sucks, her eyes wide open.
All night, she does not sleep, but does not cry.
Ike's winds howl and roar
their heavy metal lullaby:
my four-year-old sleeps, my baby eats.
My husband pushes the sofa
against our French doors
that bow slightly inside,
a push and pull dance
all night to Ike's guitar riffs.

By morning, Ike's music has played out.
The baby is tired and hot.
I fan her with cardboard,
drying off the sweat of our close feedings.
The radio announces how to help others,
where to go for ice, food, and shelter.

Knowing we are better off
than most, we pray our thanks
that the tree from our front yard
now lies in the driveway.
Then, the baby wants to nurse again.

Summer Camping
Frio River, 1982

After breakfast, we walk
through shady mesquite groves,
our father striding way ahead,
Mother lagging behind
with towels, water, camera,
a book, toys, snacks.

We wear our bathing suits
and old tennis shoes awkwardly,
Mom, Dad, Gabriel, Marcus, and I.
Ahead a cliff rises golden,
its face full of lazy angles,
trees growing out here and there.

The river is low,
a shallow ribbon of water
over brownish stones.
Gabe and I float and push around on tubes,
or walk ankle deep,
feel the current in our shoes.
Mom reads. Marcus plays
on a shore of sand and rocks,
afraid of all water that moves.
The current is loud in our ears.

Dad asks me to stand
next to a tree for a picture.
I don't smile; the sun is in my eyes.

The Women Drive to the Feminist Conference

for Mary-Ann Papageorgiou

The bartender wearing tight black pants
looks away as she takes our order.
She already knows what we want.
We stand next to her bar while coffee hisses
slowly into the glass pot, liquid thin
as the blood in our nervous limbs.
Voices pummel the dark room,
and the sharp clicks of balls hitting balls
as we pass the faceless men who stand
in shadows twisting chalk onto cues with thick fingers,
the room suddenly silent as we walk to the bathroom.
A whistle squeezes under the door.

In the mirror, we change our faces, look tougher
than leather jackets when we leave. Outside,
we ignore the wind gusting our bodies
with lewd gestures and sip the bitter coffee,
warmth that will help us get to where we need to go.

Valentine's Day
Kingsville, 1999

for my mother

I remind you of the gifts you gave to us
when we were kids. My favorite a necklace
with charms like sweetheart candies,
and messages: Love You, Be Mine.
Now, you face each holiday alone,
unsure how to find your way.
I think of ways to heal,
to busy the heart with looking beyond.

This day isn't just about couples,
I tell you, reminding myself.
I know the mantras for holiday survival,
have done this dance solo over and over.

Put your energy into yourself.
Write letters to those you love.
Start with the grandchild almost born.
Tell that baby about your grandparents,
their little houses next to the railroad,
and about riding the train. Describe your life
before Father in technicolor details:
clamdigger pants and nurse's caps.
Then, my brother as a child—that blue
jumpsuit he wore when he learned to walk—
his super straight hair and hearty laugh.
Write to him too; remember his youth
for him like only a mother can.

Your life will be better without him.
It's not the same, you will say. No.
It will never be that same awful way again.
No more going through the motions,
cards drenched with false feeling,
holidays in front of the television.

Alone is not the same as lonely.
Buy flowers, soak in the tub,
redecorate, go for a walk,
listen to the birds,

write down their songs
and learn them by heart.

Let this day remind you not of a shadowy partner,
but of better times and family lines,
of connections and laughter.

The Way of Divorce

Phone Calls
Kingsville, 1998

For months, the calls:
tías, primas, mi abuela, amigas.
Always, *Have you talked to your mother?*
How's she doing?
And my father: *your mother*
this and *your mother* that.
And then my mother:
I can't do this,
your father was lying about that.

Moving In
Houston

We start with the bedroom,
decide to put the former guest bed
opposite the closet. The dresser,
sewing machine, and desk go
against the walls. But when we
work on the bed frame,
an old metal one
with stubborn screws,
the pieces won't stay together.
Upset, Mother wants to know
why he did this to her.
The only answer I have
is to keep going.
I struggle with the bars,
force the screws to hold.
Now, it's ready.

Dinner

I offer to cook, prepare a simple meal:
fideo, blackeyed peas, corn bread, salad.
My brother sets the table. He and my mother
and I, we three sit down together, turn off the tv,
talk of simple things: family memories,
and where to hang the baby's pictures.

We Visit the Cousins After My Father Does
McAllen

Ana shakes her head like always,
saying my father lies.
Ay no, she says,
he thinks we will take his side.
And Nancy says she asked,
Why did you do this to Tía?
And, *he had nothing to say.*

Across the Border
Progresso

My mother has pesos in her pocket,
left from their vacation last year,
but everything is priced in dollares,
even lunch. She looks at rings,
crosses, pendants. She buys
a cute red dress for the baby.
Finally, she chooses a tourist
outfit, blue shorts and top
with "Mexico" in silkscreen.
She asks the price in pesos,
tips the man with a smile, says,
Your father paid for that.

Girls Night Out
Corpus Christi

We go for a walk,
my mother, my aunt, and I.
Downtown, the streets are cabled off,
and we mix with all the foot traffic
from the bars. I am the only one
with ID, but we talk our way in.
We order drinks, request songs,
dance with each other in a circle.
After that, my mother prefers to watch
from the table. She'd rather sip her drink;
she's close, but not ready to let go, I think.

Change

Sky a field of buttercups
bird the dark center of an eye
wings a wave darting
coasting without tracks
carnival ride gone mad
light too yellow and storm-wild.

Bat Bridge
Austin, 1999

for Alice Hempel

Waiting for the dark,
we gather on hills,
our chatter rising
like an invocation.
The bats we summon
still sleep, tucked
between seams
of the Congress Avenue Bridge,
lulled by thumps
of passing cars.
Then, as light fades,
wake-up flights begin.
Bats slide into the night,
smooth as fish,
not schooled,
but one by two
by three by one.

Likewise, we go,
lurch off in ones,
in groups of threes
or handholding
twos, like a team
breaking formation,
or a congregation
blessed and told
go in peace,
this bat-filled
Friday evening
our vesper,
their flights
our catharsis
at week's end.

V

reverence

Ars Poetica

"I poeti sono impossibili"
—Alessandro Carrera

Poets are impossible, you say,
the title of your book translated
in the faculty newsletter. That is all
I know of what you say about poets,
since I do not read Italian. Others say
poetry is dead, over, yesterday.

Not so. The poets are not dead.
We are forever today and always
tomorrow. A poem congeals
the was, is, could be, yet reveals
all that lies beyond and between.
Poems are more than the possible:

poets imagine all that is not.
What else but a poem could tell us
the story behind Hopper's diner,
or surmise what The Lady wrote,
wrote again in her letter while Vermeer
painted, painted her for months?

Poets are impossibly hopeful:
a poem feels, deeply, truly
sees the ocean in every tear,
hears the notes a voice may sing.
Impossibly poetic, how could a poet
believe, without metaphor or song?

The Last Stradivarius

1736, and the village of Cremona
is full of luthiers, strangers
eating thick ravioli with pepper sauce
at the inn every night, drinking chianti
as they sit at long wooden tables
discussing steam times and wood bends
in French, German, and Russian
while the innkeeper's two sons stumble to fill
every raised mug, keep every taper burning.

In the mornings, these craftsmen depart early,
their pockets stuffed with heavy rolls
baked by the innkeeper's wife.
They eat as they walk
to the luthier master's cottage,
afraid he'll begin without them,
that he'll finish the instrument
in the dark and die before they learn
the secret step he insists does not exist.

Already, they have forgotten what he said
about the sunlight, how they must never work
without seeing the sun delve
into the wood and shine back,
how the sun shows where to cut,
where to shape the curves
that become violin or cello.
He has told them to go home,
move their work benches
outside, where sun speaks to wood,
and melody forges the instrument.

Sweetness

after Naomi Shihab Nye

I visited Monmouth, Illinois, this summer for the first time, the town where my friends now live. We walked up and down the main street, visiting city offices and the overstuffed three-story gift and candy store. A study of contrasts. We drove with their dogs to the park, where the boys sniffed trees, plants, grass. *This is good exercise for the brain, all the new smells*, my friend said.

We walked, fast, the border of the park by the woods and found blackberry bushes, loaded with ripe and unripe berries. Sweet and juicy. *I love finding things no one else knows about*, he said.

Stations of the Cross Park, Mount St. Francis Friary

Ash and pine poke through sloped banks,
a vista of miniatures versus giants.

These towers crowd and disperse,
segregate one turn, one station

of the path from another,
one solemn moment from the next.

Dry and rocky creek bed,
years of leaves going soft.

Butterflies, giant black ants, bees,
and daddy longlegs spiders hover.

Locusts and cicadas hum their low chants,
lulling all who visit.

We pause, in reverence,
before we must walk on.

A Comment on Deconstruction

Still Life

Doll beside a head shot of the doll,
each wearing a white kerchief crown.
The doll is both toy and art.
The photograph is both art and symbol,
a symbol of a symbol of a symbol
and so on.

Critique

Her stare a prayer passing through
blackened windows: her four round eyes.
They plead with me, doll and photograph,
each its own voice.

Gallery

Dolls, each with a photograph,
an arm or leg or action shot.
And photographs of dolls and their photographs
together, a fugue of representation,
a cacophony of images building
to the point of collapse.

Not Pompeii

after Charles Bernstein

No, the rich men do not know about suffering,
that which rises from any thing, natural
or unnatural. Suffering is the domain
of the poor, who are not ignorant of things
beyond control: ocean waves, changing coastlines,
or their own terrible greed for the wealth of others.
Naturally, the poor envy the rich's
cornucopia. They see some progress;
others are denied. Poverty is the price
of human advancement. The fishmonger
sees his living in the faces of the trout,
sees dwindling schools in the quickly melting
ice. He cares not for ancient lava flows,
the people they buried, the poems written about them.

Spring Cleaning, 2003

On television, men hit the base of the statue.
I take down the white curtains
with the quarter moon eyelets.
Amid rejoicing, the statue topples.
I brush off a thin layer of the cats' winter fur.
The cityscape behind the statue is broken.
My curtains tumble in the washer and dryer.
A man hits the eyes of the statue with his shoe.

I spray the windows with vinegar,
wipe every smudge.
Men are looting empty buildings:
vases, Sumerian artifacts.
I iron the curtains crisp as paper.
Someone has taken
the oldest written documents.

I hang up the curtains,
tie them open at their middles.
Tablets of cuneiform on clay.
The cats look out the window.
On television: statue, city, shoe, museum.

Eight thousand years ago, a man wrote in clay.

Why Stieglitz Photographed O'Keeffe's Hands

Because careful petals
suggest the whole.

Because red hills are the sun
in muted sky.

Because a day becomes
a night and thus, goes on.

Pájaros
Kingsville, 1997

for Sara Greenslit

Sunset is bird time, when staggered checkmarks
of grackles and blackbirds arc across the sky,
looping to a different palm tree or telephone wire,
circling back to where they started, like revenge.
As they ca-caw from place to place to place,
haloing overhead, they net me with their nosiness,
with their scurries here and there and there.
What makes them anxious and talky as brand new parents?
Do they wonder where the day has gone,
marvel at the creamy sky, or simply greet endlessly,
saying, *Ca-caw, I'm here. Hello; hello.*

Aguacate

Slippery flesh that melts in my mouth,
yellow green color of new leaves,
when I squeeze your oval body
after slicing you in half,
your insides chunk off
the smooth underside of your skin,
which is so wonderfully nubbly
on the outside, as if the rain
had hardened on you while it fell.

I love to eat you whole, slice
you in half lengthwise,
remove your teardrop
pit with a flick
of the knife
and part
your flesh
into slim boats
that lay shipwrecked
on the plate, or float in a sea of lettuce,
slicking green goo onto the tomatoes.

Or, I scoop you out with a spoon
into el molcajete and mash you smooth
con chiles pequeños. Guacamole
pa' comer con tostaditas
or to spread onto a tortilla solo
con frijoles para cenar.

I enjoy you any which way,
always fresh from your skin,
the dark rind that seals you in,
your tropical taste
su sabor tropical
full flavored for my tongue.

Where the Bus Stops

In front of the library, under the old old maple tree whose remaining leaves are as big as my face, bigger, and browner too. I am waiting, swathed in coat, scarf, hat, gloves. A slight wind teases the crisp heap of fallen leaves at waist level (because the street and sidewalk cut into the slope of the hill). And I see these leaves as if for the first time, a pile of hands gone loose. They are waiting too, these autonomous hands, for strong wind, to set sail and glide away to new stops. They wait with patience learned while sprouting during spring melts, while slowly soaking the full light of summer sun, while crisping into dry crones in autumn chill. They wait here with me, under the old old maple tree in front of the library, where the bus stops.

Hope Near the End
Katy, 1998

for my brothers

Nearly August, I walked around the block with my father,
the sun low low to our right as we began,
streets widening before us as if forming with the dark.
The air, swollen with wet, made our steps heavy.
Above us, a quarter moon, bright as a window.
The neighbors' houses sat comfortable as old boulders.
In one of the yards, a sprinkler swished, everything else still still.
My father spoke of his pending retirement,
and I thought of the first grandchild
swelling in my sister-in-law's womb,
comfortable and wet in the darkness and stillness
of its days. And we walked straight into that night,
quarter moon watching like an eye,
like the barest opening of an eye.

Mist

for Bonnie Maurer

The summer drought has broken—
a warm rain fell and lingered,
like a visit from an old friend,
and now this mist glows
in the last light of the day
like the ghost of winter,
smoke rising from the ground
like breath and lingering
over hay stubble and poke berries,
over the smooth line of the path,
a gauzy softness drawn over the shoulders
of the lake like a shimmering shawl.
Cattails poke their innocent fingers up
from the edge of the water,
as if gripping at that shawl,
as if keeping still this moment,
like a communion
that continually nourishes.